BORN IN THE 30s

BORN IN THE 30s

Tim Glynne-Jones

ARCTURUS

ARCTURUS

This edition published in 2022 by
Arcturus Publishing Limited
26/27 Bickels Yard, 151–153 Bermondsey Street,
London SE1 3HA

Copyright © Arcturus Holdings Limited

ISBN: 978-1-78404-739-9
AD004583UK

Printed in China

Contents

All photographs from *Getty Images*

Introduction

• •

The 1930s will forever be remembered for two global calamities: the Great Depression and World War II. But against that grim backdrop lies an age of great advances and enlightenment, in which many of the luxuries that we take for granted today came into general use for the first time, and more liberal attitudes towards sexual and racial equality, education and the law began to evolve. This book depicts the human face of the 1930s in wonderfully evocative pictures and recollections of an exciting time in history.

The Roaring Twenties had deflated like a punctured tyre and the Great Depression had spread like a plague across the world. In Britain it hit the industrial centres like a wrecking ball, leaving whole communities out of work and forcing the mass movement of an increasingly redundant labour force, as people travelled in search of work. And there was work to be found, for while the old industries like coal mining collapsed, new technologies were springing up, such as the electronics industry, spurred on by the broadcast revolution.

For those who did have work, life had never been better. Electrical appliances like vacuum cleaners and washing machines took away the elbow grease of domestic work, over a million households owned their own car and most people went to the cinema at least once a week, enjoying the wonders of sound and Technicolor.

Workers took paid holidays for the first time, and spent them in new holiday camps at the seaside. And a general zeal for health and fitness saw an increase in outdoor activities, such as swimming at the newly opened lidos.

For children, life was improving too. Educational reforms meant more options and a better chance to further your education beyond the school leaving age of 14; though youngsters were probably less excited by that than they were about the new cosmos of chocolate bars that made their first appearance in the 1930s, Mars and Milky Way being just two of many that have survived.

But in all the excitement, there were regular reminders that all was not well. The rise of Hitler, Mussolini and Franco in Europe inspired Britain's own band of fascists, led by Oswald Mosley, which in turn sparked violent confrontations. There were also race riots and protests over major issues like women's rights and capital punishment. The monarchy was rocked, first by the death of King George V, then by the abdication scandal of Edward VIII, but the trials and tribulations at the Palace were put into stark perspective by the arrival of the Jarrow hunger marchers at Downing Street in the midst of it all.

The difference between the haves and the have-nots was marked. As the middle class aspired to private cars and washing machines, the working class struggled for food. The latter half of the decade would see a gradual improvement but only one thing could truly unite the country: a common enemy, namely Adolf Hitler.

Taking Things In Your Stride

To be a child growing up in the 1930s could have meant one of two things: a brave new world of wonder and hope, or a grim destiny of working to survive. Such was the divided nature of Britain in an age of enlightenment, played out against a backdrop of mass unemployment.

More mothers were going out to work, meaning more demand for childcare. The Nursery School Association, founded in 1923, began to exert a greater influence over the care and education of young children, and gradually the education system evolved to recognize the need to give all children proper schooling, at least until the age of 14, the national school leaving age.

In some cases, though, families were given special dispensation to take their child out of school at the age of 12 so that they could go out and earn a wage to help the family survive. Not for them the toy cars, radios and chocolate bars that their middle-class contemporaries were beginning to expect as normal. For them the way out was often through sport, at least in the imagination. Childhood was a time in which your own imagination provided the entertainment and children of all backgrounds were united by the freedom to dream.

Left *Being born in the 1930s was a perilous business. With no antibiotics available, one in 20 babies died before their first birthday, of diseases like meningitis and pneumonia. But this healthy 10-month-old has plenty to look forward to, having been pronounced 'the world's loveliest baby' by the Duchess of York.*

Right *Doubtless imagining he's a star racing driver, a little boy borrows a parental glove to steer his toy car to glory. By the 1930s, cars were widespread, having virtually driven horse-drawn transport off the highway. Of around 2.5 million motor vehicles on the road, half were private cars and road safety was a major issue.*

The horse wasn't entirely redundant, though. In agriculture it was still used extensively and agricultural shows, like this one at Horfield near Bristol, gave children the chance to come face to face with these majestic beasts, and offer them a bit of gratitude for all the food they had helped to produce in the shape of a sugar lump.

Behind-the-scenes skulduggery at a baby show sees one contestant perfecting the art of looking the other way while sabotaging the efforts of a rival. After the strict discipline of the previous decades, the 1930s saw a more liberal approach to parenting, but this sort of mischief would not have gone unpunished.

Children enjoy a ride on a merry-go-round, fitted with cars rather than horses, at Butlin's amusement park in Skegness. Billy Butlin opened his first holiday camp at Skegness in 1936 and his second, at Clacton-on-Sea, in 1938. The camps were a huge success, giving many people their first experience of a seaside holiday.

Off to Dreamland

Children at a nursery school take their afternoon nap, while their nurses enjoy the peace and quiet to read their books. The number of nursery schools in Britain doubled during the 1930s as the Nursery School Association responded to the call for children to begin their education at a younger age.

The emphasis of pre-school education was on health, nourishment and physical welfare rather than intellectual learning, the introduction of nurseries being part of a philanthropic movement to help the children of deprived communities to get a better start in life. By the 1930s about one third of British women worked outside the home, so the demand for pre-school childcare was high. Nevertheless, by 1937, half of the 87 nurseries recognized by the Board of Education were still voluntary.

Open-air nurseries were very much in vogue, encouraging children to lead an active, outdoor life that promoted health and physical development.

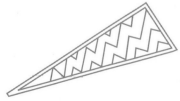

Even more exciting than the toy car was the toy aeroplane. Air travel was still in its infancy, with pioneers like Amelia Earhart still setting new records, and although the jet engine was invented in 1930, the skies were still the domain of airships and biplanes powered by propellers.

Children play outdoors at an experimental nursery school in Yorkshire. Popular outdoor toys of the time could be anything that rolled: tricycles, barrows, buggies and balls. Girls could emulate their mothers pushing imaginary prams and shopping trolleys, while boys mimicked their dads on the allotment or their sporting heroes on the football field or race track.

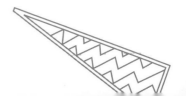

Left *A poignant encounter between two young boys and the staff and children at an orphanage in London. The care of parentless children was a major issue in the 1930s, with many orphans still being shipped to the colonies or offered up for adoption for profit, a practice outlawed by the 1939 Adoption of Children (Regulation) Act.*

Right *The 1930s was the heyday of the outdoor municipal swimming pool, or lido as it became known, from the Italian word for a beach. More than 150 lidos were built across Britain during the decade, providing people like this father and son with a taste of open-air bathing without having to go to the seaside.*

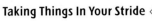

Nativity Play

Some things never change. Children at an infant school in London adopt the familiar costumes and positions of the annual Nativity play, with a toy doll for the baby Jesus.

Although religious education in schools was not yet a statutory requirement and church attendance was beginning to fall off, the 1930s saw a peak in both Anglican baptisms (seven out of every 10 newborns) and confirmations (three in 10). Sunday School was where children received their religious education. Each Sunday they would be taught a weekly prayer, or 'collect', and they would have to learn it and recite it to the teacher. Attendance was rewarded with prizes, such as a bible, for those who came most often, with attendance stamps collected over the year.

While fewer parents attended church themselves, they were keen to maintain some religious association by sending their children to Sunday School. The Nativity play was another opportunity to reconnect with the Christian beliefs which most people still professed to have.

Left *A schoolboy blocks his ears as he watches a display at the Royal Air Force Pageant at Hendon Aerodrome. The public was already spellbound by the grace and agility of aircraft and the pageant was a chance to see the most skilled pilots flying in close formation and staging mock bombing raids.*

Right *An engine driver talks to two young passengers at Euston Station. In the face of rapidly increasing competition from the roads, railway companies spent the 1930s investing in speed. The result was a dynasty of sleek, powerful locomotives and a period that will be remembered as the Golden Age of Steam.*

Ask a Policeman

A young gymkhana competitor gets directions from a local 'bobby'. The role of the police constable on the beat was pivotal to social behaviour. Children were brought up to respect the police and if they stepped out of line and broke a window or pinched the apples off someone's tree, they could expect to get a clip round the ear from a policeman. If they ran home and told their parents about it they were likely to get another smack for getting into trouble.

Young offenders could be punished with the birch but in extreme cases, anyone over the age of 16 could be hanged. In 1933 the minimum age for hanging was raised to 18.

The Great Depression did coincide with an increase in crime, including a rise in youth crime, and the rise in car-related crime meant that bobbies on bicycles were not always the ideal men for the job. Yet it remained a relatively peaceful decade, despite the gulf in relative living standards and the resentment that that might have inspired.

Children blow on the command of a conjuror, who is keeping them entertained as part of a summer holiday event on Clapham Common, organized by London County Council. Whenever the sun shone, children were encouraged to go outdoors and get some fresh air, so this kind of entertainment was hugely popular.

Song and Dance

● ●

A group of budding Fred Astaires rehearses a dance routine at Streatham Baths as part of a celebration pageant for King George V's Silver Jubilee.

On 6 May 1935, King George broadcast an address to the Empire, in which he expressed his sympathy for the millions who were out of work, and his gratitude for the love and loyalty that had been extended to him by his subjects. He also called on the young people to be ready to give to their country 'the service of your work, your time and your hearts'. Perhaps he could foresee that much more would soon be required of them.

Less than a year later the king was dead, sparking a year of monarchical turmoil during which Britain was thrown into the abdication crisis, which saw his successor, Edward VIII, choose to relinquish the crown in favour of marrying the divorcee Wallis Simpson. Thus the crown passed to Edward's brother Albert, who was crowned George VI and would reign until his death in 1952.

Music and movement classes were helped by radio broadcasts from the BBC, which became a familiar feature in schools. Across the country, children would gather round the wireless in the school hall or gymnasium and follow the instructions from Broadcasting House, learning to express themselves through movement, or something like that.

A young boxer goes through his combinations under the supervision of his dad, perhaps dreaming of one day emulating the great Welsh fighter Tommy Farr, British and Empire heavyweight champion, who took the great Joe Louis to 15 rounds in 1937 and lost narrowly on points.

Ming, one of the first giant pandas ever to land in Britain and the first baby panda, is photographed by Picture Post *photographer Bert Hardy doing the same for Hardy's son, Mike. Ming was born in 1937 and arrived from China at Christmas 1938, but lived for just six years, a popular exhibit at London Zoo during that time.*

Each year on 24 May, schoolchildren throughout the British Empire would celebrate Empire Day, a tradition that started in 1916 and would last until 1958. It was all about celebrating being sons and daughters of 'a glorious Empire' and for children like these it meant leaving school early to take part in parades and dances.

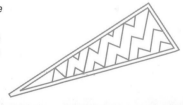

Although motor cars were rapidly growing in number and knocking people down with frightening regularity, residential streets were still a relatively peaceful playground for the neighbourhood children, who would gather to play tag or skipping or, like these children in Millwall, with London's docks in the background, play cricket using a wooden crate for stumps.

Nursery children learn the rudiments of laundering their own hankies and dusters, plus a cuddly rabbit whose ears prove particularly handy for pegging to the line. Hand washing was already becoming a thing of the past, however, as automatic washing machines were gradually beginning to appear.

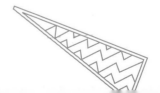

These little angels are thrilled to be on their way to a film set. Cinema was the most popular form of commercial entertainment throughout the 1930s, with 18 million people a week buying tickets to watch their idols and dream of making it to Hollywood to become a screen star.

Best Years of Our Lives

For children growing up in the 1930s there were few luxuries in life. Children were expected to fend for themselves much more than they are today and they were expected to do their bit towards keeping house too.

One in two households had a radio and it wasn't until 1936 that the BBC began television broadcasting. Even then, very few people owned a 'box'. Entertainment meant going outdoors and playing with the other neighbourhood children. Football and cricket were popular, and impromptu matches would be played in the street. As long as you were home in time for tea, your parents didn't spend their time worrying about where you were.

Bigger events included day trips to the seaside or the countryside, rubbing shoulders with school pals, workmates or neighbours in lumbering charabancs and revelling in the thrill of a change of scenery. Public entertainments were laid on in the summer in the parks and at the seaside, and increasingly popular was the open-air swimming pool, which would teem with eager bathers whenever the sun came out – and even when it didn't. No-one expected Mediterranean temperatures in those days.

School Dinners
● ●

The table may be laid as if for a banquet but the expressions on the children's faces say it all about school dinners in the 1930s. For most children, dinnertime, usually starting at midday and running until 1.30pm, meant walking home for lunch. Only about a quarter of a million children had school dinners. But for those who did, school dinnertime was a daily nightmare.

There was no choice about what you ate. Watched over by draconian dinner ladies, children would grind their way through the familiar staples of boiled cabbage, mince, lumpy mashed potato and gravy, followed by semolina or some sort of tart, washed down with beakers of warm water.

The Milk in Schools Scheme became official in the 1930s, giving children a free third of a pint a day in a glass bottle, distributed among the class by the milk monitors. The same children might also be nominated to collect the dinner money at the start of the school day, which amounted to a penny a day.

Left *Bucket, spade and dolls in hand, two girls show their excitement as they prepare to pull out of Euston Station for a Bank Holiday excursion to the seaside. For most workers in Britain, Bank Holidays were the only paid leave until the Holidays with Pay Act was passed in 1938.*

Right *Two young boys enjoy the summer sunshine as they play in the sea at Westward Ho! in Devon. The 1930s saw a large increase in the number of people taking an annual holiday to the seaside and by the end of the decade, 15 million people were going to the coast for a week or two each year.*

Discipline was strict in most schools, with corporal punishment meted out to those who misbehaved, but there was room for fun in class. Dogs in the classroom were rare, but teachers would use different methods to keep the children interested and enthused as they learnt the three Rs: reading, writing and 'rithmetic.

Fifi the chimpanzee gives a group of senior school girls a lesson in deportment as they stop for refreshments on a visit to London Zoo. The Chimpanzees' Tea Party, which was first held in 1926, became a popular daily attraction at the zoo in the 1930s.

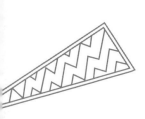

'Last one home's a sissy!' Children race out of school, clearly excited at being released, and charge home down a street in east London. These were the children of dock workers, living so close to their fathers' workplace that the ocean liner in the background appears to be part of the architecture.

Say Aaaaah

· ·

Two children wait in trepidation while a third has a check-up at a mobile dental surgery, the first of its kind in Britain, in 1931. Dental treatment was a rarity in the 1930s. At the beginning of the war, 95 per cent of army recruits were found to fall short of the required dental standard, such was the lack of treatment on offer.

Workers who opted into the National Health Insurance scheme could get dental treatment paid for by their Approved Insurance Society, but the privilege did not extend to members of their family. Free dental treatment was introduced for pregnant mothers and for their children up to the age of five, but still the majority of people did not go to the dentist, and only two-thirds of children received school dental examinations each year.

If you needed false teeth you could often pick up a set in the local market. If they didn't fit you'd put them back and try another pair. Anything to avoid the cost and the fear of taking your chances in the dentist's chair.

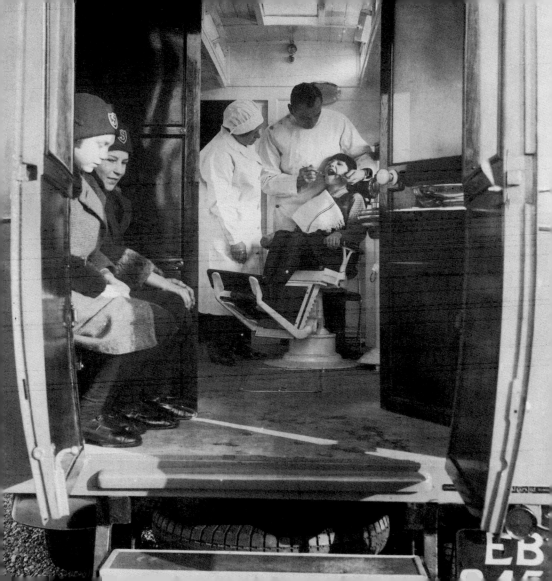

A group of schoolchildren watch the dress rehearsal of a historical outdoor festival. Such events often featured kings and queens from history on past visits to wherever the show was being held. Sometimes these pageants extolled the virtues of the Co-operative movement or the Communist party. Perhaps that's why none of the kids look too thrilled.

Four boys hit the road in Oxford. Roller skating was a popular recreation for children in the 1930s. You could buy a pair of skates for sixpence from Woolworths, strap them to the bottom of your shoes and off you'd go, hurtling down the road at high speed.

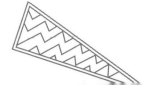

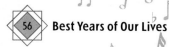

Away Day

Children pile aboard an open-top charabanc for an excursion from Bethnal Green to Epping Forest. Such communal outings, either to the seaside or the countryside, had been very popular among neighbourhood communities and work colleagues in the early part of the 20th century but, with private motor transport becoming more accessible and modern buses becoming faster and safer, the use of the charabanc began to decline in the 1930s.

Nevertheless, the large, slow, cumbersome vehicles continued to be regularly wheeled out in the summer and parked outside the local pub, where they would wait for the neighbourhood day-trippers or the factory workers to convene. On large outings it was common practice for women and men to travel in separate vehicles, the men with a barrel of beer in theirs, which usually meant a good sing-song on the journey home.

In 1907, a primary school headmistress from Bow, east London, set up a wooden arch on the pavement. Any child small enough to pass through it without bending could receive a parcel of toys for a farthing. Here are some little girls who still quallfied in 1939.

Two boys from Harrow School maintain a haughty distance as their distinctive dress causes amusement for their less well-to-do contemporaries. Britain in the 1930s was still built on a rigid class structure, with the public school-educated elite believing they had a moral superiority over the lower classes.

*A group of boys strain to get the height they need to peer into a
row of mutoscopes, also known as 'what the butler saw machines'.
The mutoscope was a coin-operated moving picture device that
was popular on piers and at amusement parks and often showed
risqué images, hence the nickname.*

Left *This family of 11 children, including five pairs of twins, bucks the trend for smaller family sizes. The average number of children in a working-class family in the 1930s was 1.8 – half of what it had been at the turn of the century, despite the falling infant mortality rate.*

Right *A class of girls from Hackney enjoy the rare pleasure of a lesson outdoors during a school holiday to the seaside at Broadstairs in Kent. The Kent coast was a popular destination for Londoners heading out to catch the sea air and dip their toes in the brine.*

You don't need to be a lip-reader to know these boys are shouting something pretty rude during a schoolboys football match at the Spotted Dog Ground, east London. The footballing heroes of the day were Arsenal, who won the league championship five times in the 1930s, and even featured in a film, The Arsenal Stadium Mystery.

A girl and her nanny practise skipping in the park.
The girl is in her summer dress but the nanny is
wearing the classic long, heavy coat, as popularized
by Mary Poppins, who first appeared in print in the
novel of the same name in 1934.

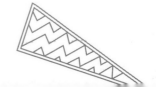

Spitting Image

The political scene of the 1930s was increasingly dominated by the sinister antics of Adolf Hitler and his Nazi party in Germany, and the determination of Britain's political leaders to pursue a policy of appeasement. Most people refused to acknowledge the threat of Hitler's movements into Austria, the Rhineland and Czechoslovakia. Others advocated fascism, notably Oswald Mosley, who formed the British Union of Fascists in 1932.

A lone dissenting voice was Winston Churchill, then a Conservative back-bencher, who spoke repeatedly about the need to curb Hitler but was generally dismissed by senior politicians who were reluctant to drag Britain into another conflict so soon after the carnage of World War I.

By 1939, however, Churchill was vindicated. Hitler became a figure of public mockery, epitomised by Charlie Chaplin who filmed *The Great Dictator* in that year. In this picture, a boy helps his friend put on a Hitler face mask, probably in preparation for a hectic game of Scrag.

During the 1930s the practice of sending poor orphaned children to the colonies to bolster the labour force was still going on, though it slowed down during this period due to the economy. These Home Children, as they were called, are waiting to board a train at Waterloo on their way to a new life in Western Australia.

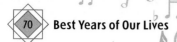

Star Pupil

●●●●●●●●●●●●●●●●●●●●●●●●●●●

This boy from Treorchy Junior Mixed School in Wales is hoisted aloft by classmates after being awarded a free place at the local secondary school, a reward for his exemplary conduct and never having been late or absent in six years.

One in five children attended secondary school in the 1930s. Bright pupils could sit an entrance exam for a scholarship to a grammar school, which would educate them in preparation for university. The statutory school leaving age was still 14, although the 1936 Education Act would raise it to 15. Where children were required to work in order to help support the family, exceptions to the new law were granted.

The elementary school system, which included all-age classes of over 60 kids, began to make way for a new primary structure, divided into infants (5 to 7), juniors (up to 11) and seniors (up to 14). Out of this came specialist primary schools, which focused on children up to the age of 11.

Left *The simple pleasures in life don't change and the combination of sun and water was a winner in the 1930s. A heatwave in London brings out the local schoolchildren, who delight in running through the spray from a fireman's hose and getting a good soaking.*

Right *A Basque refugee from the Spanish Civil War, one of nearly 4,000 children who arrived in Britain in 1937 and were accommodated for the summer in a makeshift camp at North Stoneham near Southampton. Elsewhere, Britain became home to thousands of Jewish refugees escaping the spread of Nazi Germany.*

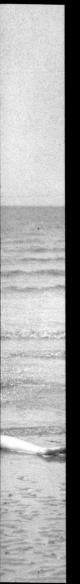

Ah, how good it is to be alive! If there was one overall theme
to life in the 1930s it was an almost scientific approach to
getting the most out of it. And science played a big part. New

Good Times

technology was creating a landscape
of invention and progress, with art
deco factories turning out vacuum cleaners, radios, washing
machines and cars in their many thousands.

Inspired by this bold leap into the future came a trend
for physical health and the outdoor life. Any opportunity
to get out of the house and do something was snapped up
eagerly, whether it was a trip to the countryside or the coast,
an afternoon in the park or a game of sport of some kind.
Healthy living went hand in hand with an interest in physical
wellbeing, both through medical advances and co-ordinated
physical exercise, conducted in large groups with almost
military precision.

Femininity was to the fore, the boyish fashions of the
1920s having given way to a more conservative, womanly
style. Hats were still de rigueur and underwear was becoming
less cumbersome, especially for the men, who celebrated the
arrival of Y-fronts in 1935.

Buttoned-up collars and cloche hats are the order of the day for the women as this family group enjoy a hot afternoon on the beach. After the flamboyant 1920s, women's dress became more conservative in the 1930s, unless you went all the way and donned your bathing suit.

This boy looks quite philosophical about losing his ice cream to a gang of donkeys at the beach in Douglas, Isle of Man. Ice cream sales boomed in the 1930s, probably due to boys asking their parents for another after losing the first one to a donkey.

The waves at Newquay in Cornwall attract a family of surfers with their narrow and short wooden boards. Bathing caps weren't just an integral part of beach fashion, they kept the hair salt-free and out of the eyes. Men, of course, didn't need them, the long, blond surfer hairdo being several decades away.

Spot the tea bar! Yes, this mobile café leaves nothing to chance, supplying trippers on Blackpool beach with their vital refreshment. Apart from the little girl, most people are dressed for a vicar's tea party in October, the men in suits and ties, the women in calf-length frocks, as was deemed proper.

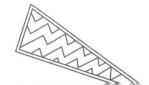

Penny for the Guy!

· ·

Remember remember the fifth of November
Gunpowder, treason and plot.
I see no reason why gunpowder treason
Should ever be forgot

Forget Halloween, Guy Fawkes Night was the big autumn event for children in the 1930s. These effigies are rather high-class examples of the 'Guys' constructed, often weeks in advance, and then put on public display with a child or two sitting next to them, free from parental scrutiny, crying, 'Penny for the Guy!'

Not many Guys wore early 16th century English dress like this. The most important thing was that they burned easily. Because at the end of the day on 5 November, the Guys would end up on a bonfire while fireworks lit up the sky behind them. The story of Guy Fawkes and the Gunpowder Plot was well known by all children and, while the pennies they collected may have been spent on sweets, it was the tradition and the thrill of the pyrotechnics that really brought Guy Fawkes Night to life.

Bunting hangs across the road and groups of grown-ups watch in amusement as children fill the streets in celebration of King George V's silver jubilee in 1935. Millions of people turned out across the country to cheer, but critics railed at the expense of such an event at a time of severe financial depression.

Rosebud in Bloom

• •

Dance was all the rage in the 1930s as the general mood swung from depression to expression and any opportunity to get on the floor and move was taken up with great enthusiasm. The jazz and swing craze of the 1920s continued to evolve, yielding new dances like the jitterbug, which sent the dance floors into a frenzy of wriggling bodies.

Meanwhile, on the big screen, American choreographer Busby Berkeley was pushing the boundaries of cinematography with his signature style of kaleidoscopic dance routines, involving groups of girls moving in geometrical patterns, filmed from above to spectacular effect.

Perhaps inspired by Busby Berkeley and films like *Gold Diggers of 1933*, the dancers here perform a 'rosebud in bloom'. Throughout the 1930s there was great passion for 'synchronized movement and dance' across Europe, which was seen as a metaphor for what could be done if everybody pulled together. Irked, Berkeley always denied that there was any underlying political message in his work.

Roma Gypsies became a more common sight as they fled to Britain to escape the rising tensions in Europe and persecution at the hands of the Nazis. They weren't exactly welcomed with open arms as they made their home on common land but their painted wagons became objects of general curiosity.

The magic of the FA Cup grips these Tottenham Hotspur supporters as they embark at Euston on an away day to see their team play Everton in the fifth round. It was a decade that began with the first World Cup and ended with the introduction of compulsory shirt numbering.

Action! In 1935, two years before the first football match was screened live on BBC television, a film crew from the Gaumont British Picture Corporation practises the art of capturing sport on camera, as a group of Surrey schoolboys enact a typical goalmouth melée.

A typical scene on FA Cup semi-final day, 1933. The empties are stacking up at the front of the terrace and these West Ham fans appear to be having a wonderful day out, despite their team losing 2–1 to Everton. Drinking beer at the match was not only allowed, it was almost a requirement!

Mild Mannered

• •

Beer was subjected to some hefty tax increases between the wars, which brought about a change in image for this traditional working-class thirst-quencher. No longer the cheap staple, it drove drinkers to become more discerning about the quality of the beer they were drinking. In the 1930s, this in turn took it into circles, such as theatres and ballrooms, that had traditionally been the preserve of wine and spirits, and thus the consumption of beer became more widespread throughout society, even if the average consumption per head fell a little.

In response to an increase in the tax on beer in 1931, the brewers reduced the strength of their most popular beers so they could keep the price stable at 6d. When the tax was reduced again in 1933, they kept the beer the same but reduced the price to 5d. Lager was coming into Britain from Europe but the most popular tipple by far among the British public was Ordinary Mild, which these elderly friends appear to be enjoying, along with a glass of sherry.

On the Buses

In 1933, London Transport was formed in an amalgamation of the capital's tram, bus, Tube and trolleybus operators. These operators had all established a reputation for looking after their staff. Transport workers enjoyed days out, activities, classes and social events organized by their employers, as well as subsidized sports facilities that brought otherwise inaccessible pastimes within their reach.

London Transport was careful to maintain this tradition. In this picture, hundreds of children are boarding buses for the annual Transport Workers Children's Outing. The outing took children from London's working-class neighbourhoods for a day out in the countryside, offering them a rare glimpse of greenery.

The double-decker buses seen here had grown rapidly in popularity since their introduction in 1923, having the flexibility to adapt their route to London's ever-expanding suburban destinations in a way that the trams and trolley-buses could not.

'Toffee Apple and Peanut King' Billy Pearce joins Miss Irene Dipper, 'Queen of the Lambeth Walk', for a right royal knees-up as Lambeth Walk fever grips Britain and Europe following the song's success in the 1937 West End musical Me and My Girl.

A Pearly King and his little Pearly Prince share a drink at the Costers Pony and Donkey Show in Regent's Park, while their dog relaxes on the back of the donkey. Henry Croft, who started the Pearly tradition, died in 1930 and a memorial to him was unveiled in St Pancras Cemetery in 1934.

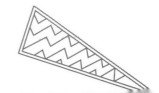

Each year, thousands of
Cockneys would board trains
from London Bridge station to the
hop fields of Kent, to earn money
picking the summer crop. Whole
families would pitch in, working
10-hour days and celebrating at
the end with a bawdy sing-song
in the local pub.

Anyone for a Smoke?
● ●

These two young women lighting up after a game of tennis show how fashionable smoking was in the 1930s. This was the decade in which women became free to light up in public. Up until then it had been considered improper but a combination of factors changed all that. One was the tobacco industry, which saw women as the great untapped market and, through its marketing divisions, began to present smoking as glamorous in order to attract female customers.

Their campaign was helped no end by the rise of Hollywood and the movie star. Iconic actresses such as Bette Davis and Greta Garbo did their bit to help glamorize cigarettes and other public figures joined the bandwagon. Eleanor Roosevelt was labelled as 'the first woman to smoke in public'. Classes were given in 'Ladies' Smoking Etiquette', which included making sure there were plenty of ashtrays and matches for dinner guests, but as time went on women mostly did it their way and felt less abashed about smoking in front of men.

They bred them tough in the East End of London. And here's how. A makeshift boxing ring strung up between the walls of houses in Poplar hosts two young pugilists, sparring for the entertainment of their peers while being watched eagerly by the two men in the foreground.

In February 1937, the country was covered in snow. On Hampstead Heath, a father dressed for the daily commute is cajoled into a toboggan ride with his two children, neither of whom has seen fit even to cover up their knees, let alone don sensible snow gear!

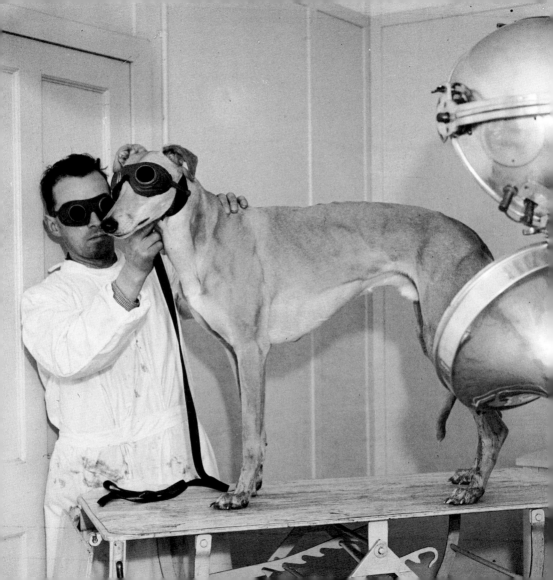

Left *Ultraviolet light, or 'artificial sunlight', treatment was a popular remedy for everything from rickets to malfunctioning dogs. The big metal lamps and rubber goggles to protect the eyes from the powerful UV rays were familiar contraptions in the surgeries of all forward-thinking medics.*

Right *Even children got in on the smoking craze, although in most cases they were restricted to lighting the thing rather than actually smoking it. Ever since the 1908 Children Act, the sale of tobacco to children under the age of 16 had been illegal as it was believed to stunt their growth.*

Having fun in large groups was the natural way of things. Given the proliferation of women in the photograph, we can only assume they are being entertained by some contest for the men out on the grass as they enjoy the comforts and amenities of Butlin's Holiday Camp in Skegness.

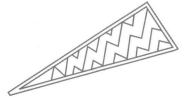

*How many soldiers does it take to move a piano? Enough
in this case, it seems, as volunteers from the 56th London
Divisional Royal Engineers wheel out the old upright and
celebrate the end of their summer training at Rottingdean,
Sussex, with a raucous sing-song outside their tent.*

Left *Health and fitness were very much on the agenda, with classes often taking the form of large groups performing choreographed exercises to music. This is a group of women teachers, of whom there was a large increase in numbers due to better education opportunities.*

Right *Women were eager to embrace any innovations that might come their way and this fairground reveller at Southend is inadvertently showcasing one of the most popular development areas of the late-1930s: nylon – first used for toothbrushes in 1938 and then replacing silk in the manufacture of stockings.*

With grim relish, a group of women gather outside the court in Manchester for the double murder trial of Dr Buck Ruxton, who was hanged for killing his wife and housemaid. It was one of the most infamous cases of the age and one of the first murder cases to be successfully proven using forensics.

Just to prove that you're never too old to get out
and have fun, the Victoria Dock Mission organized
an annual outing to Walton-on-the-Naze for the
grandmothers of the East End. Heaven knows what
mischief this lot are about to get up to.

Now there's something you don't see every day, and you didn't in the 1930s either. This man has made a special sidecar so he can take his pet lion on the wall of death. It's hard to tell whether the lion is enjoying the wind-in-the-mane thrill of it all or hanging on for dear life.

Like sentinels on the English coast looking across the Channel to the gathering storm in Europe, four men put the diving boards on the seafront at Ramsgate to an alternative purpose, taking advantage of their height to do a spot of fishing without getting soaked by the waves.

The Way We Were

Political upheaval rampaged throughout the 1930s, with battle lines being drawn up on many fronts: rich v poor, women v men, fascists v communists, motorists v pedestrians. What was it that brought so many issues to a head? Amidst the economic hardship and the news of horrors being perpetrated in Europe, there was a sense that these battles could be won and the time had come to fight. The old order was changing, the class system being challenged and the accepted traditions of the Empire held up to scrutiny.

And spilling out from this ethical battlefield came a hunger for progress, for beauty and entertainment, a desire to cast off the sackcloth and ashes and don the glamorous attire of Hollywood. Cinema was the weekly opium of the masses, the escape into comedy, romance, adventure or just the pure spectacular, and the thirst for entertainment was unquenchable.

Activities were carried out in groups, of neighbours, workmates or like-minded individuals, enjoying each other's company and the vigorous power of collective endeavour. And as the decade drew to a close, that collective spirit would stand the nation in good stead.

An extended family gathers for tea in a house in Whitechapel, east London. Sitting down together for the evening meal was the normal custom, a time when all the generations could discuss the events of the day, learn from each other's experiences, offer friendly advice and argue about who'd hidden grandad's teeth.

Evicted tenants in Lambeth, south London, load their belongings on to costermongers barrows. The unemployment crisis led to a high rate of homelessness, putting severe strain on the Public Assistance system, which had replaced the workhouse system after its abolition in 1930.

Billingsgate Fish Market, London in 1933:
this bustling market was famous for the early
hours kept by the fishmongers and the ripe
language they used. George Orwell worked
there in the 1930s, as did the Kray twins in
the 1950s. In 1982, it relocated to the Isle of
Dogs, a few miles down the River Thames.

Left *Hunger marchers from Jarrow play harmonicas to keep their spirits up as they make their month-long procession to London from the North-East to petition Prime Minister Ramsay MacDonald. The march was a protest against the unemployment and poverty being suffered by people in the North-East during the Great Depression.*

Right *A miner kisses his wife during a strike in 1936. The tough economic climate hit hard in the mining communities, prompting strikes for better conditions and pay. In response to falling exports in the 1920s, mine owners had enforced longer working hours and cut wages and many miners had been forced out of work. In the space of 10 years the mining workforce had been reduced by more than a third.*

Left *Pilots and aircrew at Hatfield Aerodrome enjoy the new recreation facilities with their wives, while two of their colleagues fly in. The aerodrome was built by de Havilland in 1930 and became a thriving factory and later an important airbase during the war.*

Right *The sight of young women out drinking in pubs, rubbing shoulders at the bar with men, had become commonplace by the end of the 1930s. Favourite tipples might include a sherry or a whisky and soda, as appears to be the case with this group in a bar in Douglas, Isle of Man.*

Possibly inspired by Judy Guinness, of the Guinness dynasty, who won a silver medal at the 1932 Olympics in Los Angeles, fencers from the Lyons Club go through their lunges on the roof of Lyons Corner House in Coventry Street, London, watched by waitresses, or 'Nippies', in the familiar Lyons uniforms.

Prize-winning Sealyham terriers calmly take the acclaim at Crufts Dog Show in 1930. The decade was a momentous one for the increasingly popular Crufts, which topped the 10,000 entries mark in 1936, its 50th year, but lost its founder, Charles Cruft, two years later, at the age of 86.

The pudding is presented to a group of friends who are having a smoke between courses during their Christmas party aboard a London, Midland and Scottish train. Turkey was then the popular favourite for Christmas lunch, though a small group like this might be more likely to go for goose or some other game bird.

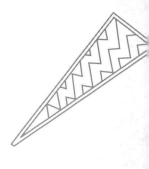

The life of a film star wasn't all glamour. 1930s slapstick favourites Laurel and Hardy (aka Arthur Stanley Jefferson and Oliver Hardy) find themselves waist-deep in a muddy puddle during filming of their 1932 film Towed in a Hole, *which was released on New Year's Eve.*

All for One

The Tiller Girls were among the most popular entertainment acts of the 1930s. Formed in 1890 by theatrical director John Tiller, they had grown into an international phenomenon, with different troupes performing all over the world. Their style of dance was known as 'fancy dancing' and later 'precision dancing', due to the uniformity of all the girls in size and shape and the precision with which they matched each other's taps and high kicks. One critic of the time said, 'They dance as one woman… and what a woman!'

But you had to be tough to make the grade. Dancers were known to be carried home from rehearsals because their feet were so sore.

Musical theatre was still largely dominated by song and dance revues and showgirls, but the decade also saw the growing influence of Cole Porter, the Gershwin brothers, and Rodgers and Hart, with sophisticated productions like *Anything Goes*, *Porgy and Bess* and *On Your Toes*.

For the upper echelons of society, public school was where you received your education and preparation for life among the ruling classes. These boys at Eton prove that you can have your cake and eat it as they mill around the tuck shop during a break in lessons.

While electric fires and central heating systems were beginning to come in, most homes were heated by coal fires, meaning plenty of work for the chimney sweeps. This firm from Deptford in south-east London have found the most efficient way to make a clean dash through the London traffic.

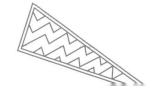

Left *A model of deportment, this aspiring fashion model is being trained to walk up steps while maintaining the correct posture. The most successful models could earn good money and lead a glamorous lifestyle, but it was hard work. They often sat around in fashion houses all day waiting to go out and show the clothes.*

Right *Despite numerous Smoke Abatement Acts passed by Parliament, the most recent in 1926, smogs continued to hit Britain's industrial cities, especially London, where the smoke from domestic coal fires continued to create pollution, immune from the regulations governing industry. The mixture of smoke and fog could reduce visibility to zero.*

Left *The* Princess
Louise *was an express
passenger steam
locomotive designed
by William Stanier and
built at Crewe in 1935
which regularly ran from
London to Carlisle. It was
withdrawn from service
in 1961. Here, a member
of the Berkhamsted
Riding School tests her
steed for speed against
the 'Iron horse'.*

Right *Not all inventions
of the 1930s were a
roaring success. The
smoking umbrella,
for example, which
sheltered your cigarette
(but not you) from
the rain, and the gas
shooting riot car were
both consigned to the
dustbin of history, as was
this ambitious project:
the KangruSpringShu,
designed to put that
extra spring in your step.*

The Sun Has Got His Hat On

A group of attendants from Metropole Cinemas tan themselves in the glow of a sunray lamp while a nurse ensures they don't get overexposed. In a country that spent much of its time under a blanket of cloud and smog, it was easy to conclude that a lack of sunlight lay at the root of many ailments – particularly if your patients worked all year round in a darkened cinema – and thus sunray treatment was advocated by many doctors, particularly for skin-related diseases.

There were many advances made in medicine, as cures were sought for polio, tuberculosis and cancer – the major scourges of the time. The invention of the electron microscope helped the cause and the discovery of radioisotopes paved the way for new cancer treatments. The 1930s also saw the first vaccines for yellow fever and typhus, the first heart-lung machine and the first blood bank – in Chicago.

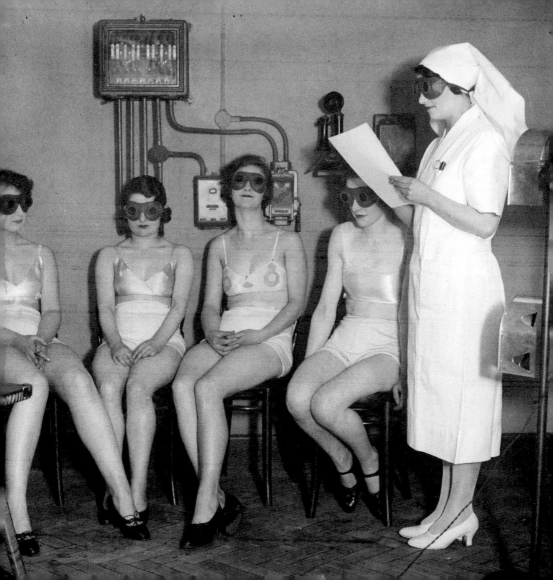

Left *This can surely only end one way. Reminiscent of the early days of manned flight, a stuntman is launched through the air in a customized plane at Alexandra Palace. Presumably there is some kind of soft landing area just out of shot.*

Right *A giant periscope at Moore Place Golf Club in Esher, Surrey, enables golfers to see if the course is clear for them to play. The 1930s saw the inauguration of the US Masters, higher prize money, more professionals and an evolution from wooden to steel-shafted clubs, bringing about a general improvement in playing standards.*

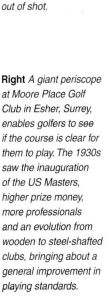

As the decade drew to an end and war with Germany became inevitable, the British public began to make provisions for possible invasion and attack from the air. The issue of gas masks began in earnest, with 38 million distributed by the time war was declared on 3 September 1939.

With the gloves now off, Britain's cities braced themselves for bombing raids by the Luftwaffe. In response to the stark message 'Dig or Die', members of a London community opt to dig an air raid shelter on a patch of waste ground near their homes, an initiative that would prove vital during the Blitz.

Two young women, their gas mask boxes hanging from their shoulders like fashion accessories, give a soldier from the British Expeditionary Force a passionate send-off at the station as he prepares for deployment in France. The war would not start in earnest until the following May and this soldier is making the most of his final moments of freedom.